# JACOBEE AND THE SCOUT PATROL

**Frannie Laurie**

Copyright © 2023
All Rights Reserved
ISBN:978-1-916954-85-4

What lays the most eggs a day?
If you know, will you say?

Let me tell you what I mean.
The answer is our very own Queen!

2,000 eggs a day she lays,
To attend to her needs, she must have maids.

Then one day they told the Queen,
Our supply of honey is very lean.

She then called for the Scout Patrol.
But where their leader was, they did not know.

The Queen ordered every Scout,
"Search here and there and round-about".

"We must have nectar for our hive,
And pollen too, so we can thrive!"

"The winner of this special quest,
Will be rewarded for doing best!"

Off they flew, they must make haste.
Flying here and there, not a minute to waste!

To find the honey not by chance,
The Bees speak through the *Waggle Dance!*

Then it was time for Jacobee,
To do his dance for all to see.

Left turn, Right turn,
Honey Bee Hop.
Right turn, Left turn,
Time to Stop!

The winner was plain to see,
None other than Jacobee!

The Queen announced to all the hive,
"Because of Jacobee, they would survive!"

As a reward, his new role,
Would be the leader of *THE SCOUT PATROL!!!*

*THE END!*

Hello friends, if you please,
Have some fun while helping Bees!

Plant some flowers and as you know,
This will help our hives to grow!

www.ingramcontent.com/pod-product-compliance
Lightning Source LLC
Chambersburg PA
CBHW040201100526
44591CB00001B/9